W9-CDL-336

WHERE ARE WE GOING IN SPACE?

by David J. Darling

Illustrated by Jeanette Swofford

DILLON PRESS, INC.   MINNEAPOLIS, MINNESOTA

The photographs are reproduced through the courtesy of the Jet Propulsion Laboratory of the California Institute of Technology and the National Aeronautics and Space Administration.

© 1984 by Dillon Press, Inc. All rights reserved

Dillon Press, Inc., 242 Portland Avenue South
Minneapolis, Minnesota 55415

Printed in the United States of America

Library of Congress Cataloging in Publication Data

Darling, David J.
    Where are we going in space?

    Summary: Traces the history of space
exploration describing the kinds of artificial
satellites and their uses.
    1. Astronautics—Juvenile literature 2. Outer
space—Exploration—Juvenile literature.
[1. Astronautics. 2. Outer space—Exploration] I. Title.
TL793.D37   1984   522   84-12672
ISBN 0-87518-265-8 (lib. bdg.)

1 2 3 4 5 6 7 8 9 10 91 90 89 88 87 86 85 84

HOLY SPIRIT LIBRARY

Contents

 **Spaceflight Facts**

Event	Spacecraft	Country	Launch Date
First artificial satellite	*Sputnik 1*	USSR	Oct 4, 1957
First animal in space (the dog Laika)	*Sputnik 2*	USSR	Nov 3, 1957
First big discovery in space (that of the earth's radiation belts)	*Explorer 1*	USA	Jan 31, 1958
First communications satellite	*Score*	USA	Dec 18, 1958
First spacecraft to escape earth's gravity pull	*Luna 1*	USSR	Jan 2, 1959
First probe to hit the moon	*Luna 2*	USSR	Sep 12, 1959
First photographs of the moon's far side	*Luna 3*	USSR	Oct 4, 1959
First weather satellite	*TIROS 1*	USA	Apr 1, 1960
First human spaceflight (by Yuri Gagarin)	*Vostok 1*	USSR	Apr 12, 1961
First successful Venus fly-by	*Mariner 2*	USA	Aug 12, 1962
First woman in space (Valentina Tereshkova)	*Vostok 6*	USSR	Jun 16, 1963
First successful Mars fly-by	*Mariner 4*	USA	Nov 28, 1964

Event	Spacecraft	Country	Launch Date
First spacewalk (by Alexei Leonov)	*Voskhod 2*	USSR	Mar 18, 1965
First probe to hit another planet (Venus)	*Venera 3*	USSR	Nov 16, 1965
First soft-landing on the moon	*Luna 9*	USSR	Jan 31, 1966
First human landing on the moon	*Apollo 11*	USA	Jul 16, 1969
First successful soft-landing on Venus	*Venera 7*	USSR	Aug 17, 1970
First space station	*Salyut 1*	USSR	Apr 19, 1971
First Jupiter fly-by	*Pioneer 10*	USA	Mar 2, 1972
First Saturn fly-by	*Pioneer 11*	USA	Apr 5, 1973
First Mercury fly-by	*Mariner 10*	USA	Nov 3, 1973
First successful soft-landing on Mars	*Viking 1*	USA	Aug 20, 1975
First flight of space shuttle	*Columbia*	USA	Apr 12, 1981
First spacewalk using a jetpack	*Challenger*	USA	Feb 7, 1984

Questions & Answers About Spaceflight

Q. Who was the first person in space?
A. Yuri Gagarin. In his *Vostok 1* capsule, he completed one full orbit of the earth on April 12, 1961. Alan Shepard, the first American in space, flew 117 miles into space aboard the *Freedom 7* capsule on May 5, 1961.

Q. What is the farthest that astronauts have ever traveled on the moon?
A. Using their lunar rover, *Apollo 17* astronauts Cernan and Schmidt covered a total distance of 18 miles (29 kilometers).

Q. Have the United States and the Soviet Union ever teamed up in space?
A. Yes. In July 1975, an American Apollo capsule, carrying three astronauts, and a Soviet Soyuz capsule, carrying two cosmonauts, linked together in orbit around the earth.

Q. Who was the first American spacewoman?
A. Dr. Sally Ride, who flew with the seventh space shuttle mission in June 1983. Twenty years earlier, Valentina Tereshkova became the first spacewoman of all when she orbited the earth in *Vostok 6*.

Q. Which was the most powerful rocket ever built?
A. The Saturn 5, which launched the Apollo spacecraft to the moon. It had a thrust, at lift-off, of 7½ million pounds (3½ million kilograms).

Q. How fast does a spacecraft have to go to escape the earth's gravity?
A. About 25,000 miles per hour (40,000 kilometers per hour).

Q. On what other worlds have spacecraft landed so far?
A. The moon, Venus, and Mars.

Q. Which has been the most difficult planet to explore?
A. Venus. It's the hottest world in the solar system and is surrounded by a crushing atmosphere. No probe has survived for more than an hour on its hot, rocky surface.

Q. Which were the first spacecraft to look for life on another planet?
A. The Viking landers. They tested for life on the surface of Mars in 1976.

Q. When did the first spacecraft leave the solar system?
A. June 13, 1983. On that date, *Pioneer 10* went farther from the sun than any planet and entered the space between the stars.

Q. What was the first satellite repaired from the space shuttle?
A. The Solar Maximum mission probe, a satellite launched in 1980 to study the sun.

SPACE SHUTTLE LIFT-OFF FROM
CAPE CANAVERAL, FLORIDA

1 The Great Adventure

On December 7, 1872, Her Majesty's Ship *Challenger* sailed from the port of Sheerness, England, on a great adventure. The ship's mission was to explore the oceans—to measure their depth and discover what strange creatures they might contain.

Three and a half years and 79,000 miles later, *Challenger* returned. Its voyage had been a success! Hundreds of undreamed of animals and plants had been found, and some of the deepest ocean trenches had been charted. Fifty big books were needed in which to tell of all the ship's wonderful discoveries.

Today, a new *Challenger* has set sail. It has journeyed, not upon the oceans of the world, but into space. It's a member of the small fleet of **space shuttles***that's preparing for our next great adventure.

Even before the space shuttle, we have explored the world nearest to our own. Twelve astronauts have walked on the **moon.** Others have lived for weeks or months aboard **space stations** going round the earth.

Our robot probes have landed on the neighboring **planets, Venus** and **Mars,** and have skimmed by the icy giants, **Jupiter** and **Saturn.** Even now, a spacecraft is bound for the distant worlds of **Uranus** and **Neptune.**

*Words in **bold type** are explained in the glossary at the end of this book.

Others are speeding out of the sun's kingdom into the lonely space between the stars.

Why are we sending people and machines on such dangerous journeys? Why don't we stay home on earth?

First, we like to explore. We have visited almost every strange place that our own world has to offer. Now, for new adventures, we must go beyond the earth.

There are other reasons for going into space. From high above the earth, we can look back on our planet and learn a great deal about it. We can bounce messages back and forth between any two points on its surface. We can look outwards, from above the atmosphere, and see distant stars and galaxies more clearly.

Already, our use of space is important to us. But in the future, it will become even more so.

From space we can look back on our planet and learn a great deal about it. This beautiful photograph of earth was taken from the *Apollo 17* spacecraft.

As the earth's natural resources—its supply of such things as coal, oil, and metals—begin to run low, we must find new ways to obtain energy and materials. All our energy may one day come from the sun through great solar power stations in the sky. Our raw materials may come from the moon or even from the **asteroids.**

At the same time, many people will travel into space. They will live in space stations above the earth, or on other worlds in the sun's kingdom. In time, people will be born in space. To them, earth will seem a strange world.

In the distant future, starships may voyage through the deep oceans of space. They will carry the first **interstellar** pioneers. Like the *Challenger* of long ago, they may return with tales of many new and exciting things. Let's see now how this great adventure is beginning.

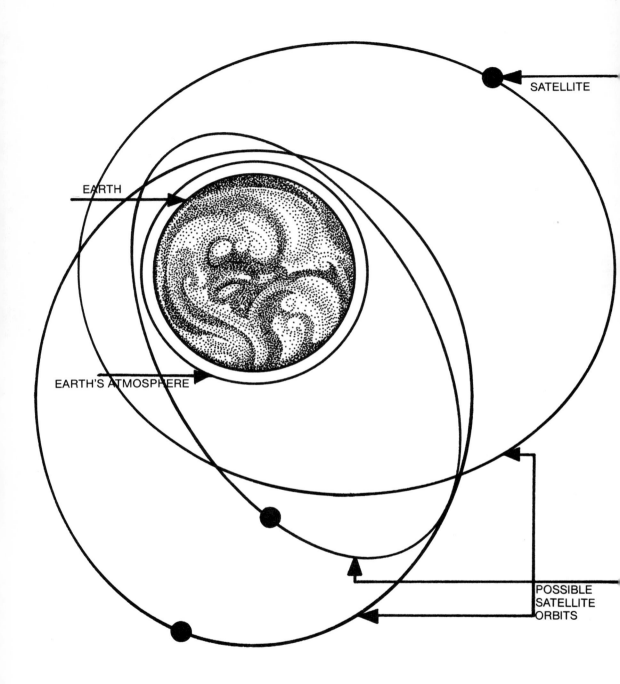

SATELLITE

EARTH

EARTH'S ATMOSPHERE

POSSIBLE
SATELLITE
ORBITS

This diagram shows some of the many possible orbits that satellites follow as they travel at high speeds around the earth. Some orbits are circular, while others are oval-shaped, or elliptical.

2 At the Edge of Space

Surrounding the earth is a sea of gases called the **atmosphere.** We live at the bottom of this sea. But just 60 miles (100 kilometers) or so above our heads, the atmosphere thins out to nothing more than a trace. If we could take a car and drive straight upwards for an hour, we'd come to the edge of space.

For many years, scientists dreamed of firing an object so high and so fast that it would travel around the earth above the atmosphere. The object would be a human-made **satellite.** Its path—like that of earth's natural satellite, the moon—would be an oval-shaped **orbit.**

On October 4, 1957, the dream came true. The Soviet Union's 184-pound *Sputnik 1* became the first human-made satellite, and the first true spacecraft. As it orbited the earth once every 90 minutes, its tiny radio transmitters sent out a steady "beep, beep." That was the sound of the Space Age being born.

Many more satellites were launched during the next few years. On November 3, 1957, *Sputnik 2* carried the first living creature into space—the dog Laika. On January 31, 1958, America's *Explorer 1* discovered huge radiation belts surrounding our planet. People began to realize just how useful orbiting spacecraft could be.

On January 31, 1958, *Explorer 1* became the first U.S. satellite in orbit around the earth. The 18-pound spacecraft discovered the Van Allen Radiation Belt. This photograph shows a model of *Explorer 1* in a space environment.

Earth Surveillance Satellites

From hundreds of miles above the earth, a satellite has a wonderful "bird's eye" view of our planet. With the right instruments, it can be used to study the land, the oceans, or the atmosphere, in great detail.

Today, **earth surveillance satellites,** equipped with special cameras and telescopes, are helping us learn more about the planet we live on. There are two main kinds.

Resource satellites study the earth's surface. They show the condition of crops and forests, or where to look for new supplies of important fuels, minerals, and metals. They also show the way the surface of our planet is made, the way its oceans move, and the places where people have built their cities and industries.

Weather satellites, on the other hand, study the at-

These two photographs were taken from *Skylab 3*, an American space station, in 1973. The photo on the left shows the New York City area, including parts of Long Island, New Jersey, and Connecticut. The photo on the right shows Hurricane Ellen over the Atlantic Ocean.

mosphere. They can spot a hurricane forming over the sea, and warn us before it strikes land. By sending back thousands of pictures every day, they help us make better and longer-range weather forecasts than ever before.

Communications Satellites

A spacecraft high above the earth can also help to send messages over very long distances. Today, there are dozens of **communications satellites** in space. Some are used to send telephone calls while others are used to send television signals. It's now possible to pick up "satellite TV" shows broadcast live from many different parts of the world.

To be useful, a communications satellite must be in a very special orbit—the **geostationary orbit**—about

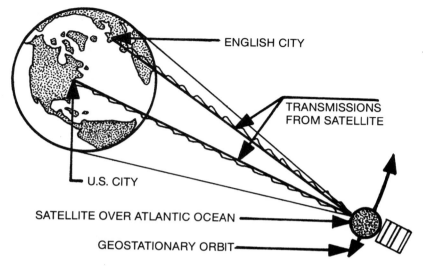

ENGLISH CITY

TRANSMISSIONS
FROM SATELLITE

U.S. CITY

SATELLITE OVER ATLANTIC OCEAN

GEOSTATIONARY ORBIT

In this drawing, a communications satellite in a geostationary orbit over the Atlantic Ocean transmits TV signals from an English city to a U.S. city. Because the satellite stays so high above the earth, it can beam signals to places that are thousands of miles apart.

22,200 miles (35,700 kilometers) above the earth's equator. This orbit allows it to stay over the same point on the earth's surface at all times. Only a certain number of satellites, though, will fit into the geostationary orbit before their signals start to get mixed up! Nations are now trying to decide how best to share this precious ring of space in the future.

Astronomy Satellites

One of the most exciting uses of earth satellites is to study distant parts of the universe. By carrying telescopes and other instruments into orbit, **astronomy satellites** can see faraway objects, such as stars and galaxies, much more clearly than we can from the earth. They can also see these objects in new ways—in **infrared**

This is an artist's view of the Space Telescope as it is launched from a space shuttle orbiter. Future astronomy satellites such as this one will be able to study objects in space far more distant than those seen by instruments on earth.

and **ultraviolet, X rays** and **gamma rays.**

Spacecraft such as the second *High Energy Astronomy Observatory* and the more recent *Infrared Astronomy Satellite* have made some important discoveries. They have found stars that give off "bursts" of X rays, an object that may be a **black hole,** and rings of warm dust around the stars Vega and Formalhaut. These rings look like new systems of planets in the making.

Soon to be launched is the **Space Telescope,** the most important astronomy satellite to date. Perched in its 300-mile-high orbit, it will be able to see objects 100 times fainter than those we can see from earth.

The Space Telescope may be joined, over the next few years, by other new satellites. The *Gamma-Ray Observatory* would study objects of great force and active power.

The *Cosmic Background Explorer* would look for signals from the beginning of the universe. And the *Advanced X-ray Astronomy Facility* would search the vast regions of space for X rays given off by distant objects. We can only imagine the amazing sights these powerful eyes in space may see.

"We Have Lift-Off!"

Putting a satellite into orbit takes a mighty force that lifts it off the earth at high speed. Imagine carrying an object, perhaps weighing a ton or more, so high and fast that it goes around the earth without ever coming down. How can it be done? The answer is with a rocket.

Burning special fuel and shooting hot gases out behind it, a rocket gives a very powerful lift. Unlike aircraft

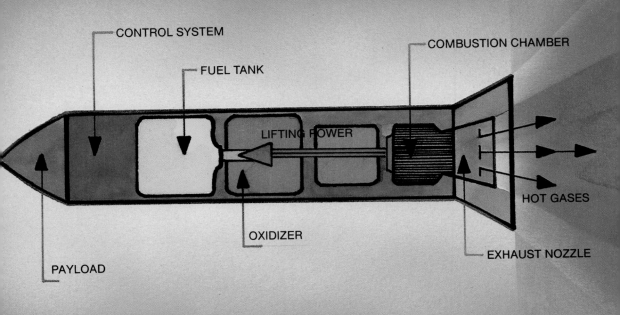

CONTROL SYSTEM

FUEL TANK

COMBUSTION CHAMBER

LIFTING POWER

OXIDIZER

HOT GASES

PAYLOAD

EXHAUST NOZZLE

This drawing shows the parts of a rocket. At lift-off burning fuel in the rocket's combustion chamber turns into hot gases. The gases expand and push hard against the front and sides but can't get out. They escape out of the exhaust nozzle. The difference between the pressure of the hot, expanding gases inside the rocket and the lower pressure outside pushes the rocket ahead.

or balloons, it can also work above the atmosphere. But a rocket can be wasteful. Once it has burned its fuel and launched its payload, it falls back to earth and is destroyed.

It would be better if we could use a spacecraft over and over again. For this reason, the Space Transportation System, or space shuttle, was built. Part rocket, part airplane, it can carry satellites into orbit, yet still return safely to land on a runway. The shuttle is made up of three parts—a 154-foot fuel tank, two solid rocket boosters, and an orbiter that takes astronauts and cargo into space. After an orbiter lands, it can be fitted out for its next mission and blasted off into space again just a few weeks later. The shuttle's twin rocket boosters are parachuted down to earth and are also used on future missions.

After a successful first mission, the space shuttle orbiter *Columbia* lands at Edwards Air Force Base in California. The short-winged orbiter is designed to fly like a silent airplane as it enters the earth's atmosphere before landing.

Living and Working in Space

During each shuttle mission, three, four, five, or more astronauts live and work aboard the orbiter for several days to a week. In space, they open the payload bay doors that protect the shuttle's valuable cargo. Using a robot arm, the astronauts release satellites that are later boosted into their correct orbits. They can even repair satellites, launched years ago, that have stopped working or have drifted from their proper paths.

One of the most exciting uses of the shuttle is to carry the European **Spacelab** into orbit. Spacelab is a space laboratory that rides inside the shuttle's cargo bay. From it scientists can study the earth, our neighborhood of space, the sun, or more distant parts of the universe in ways they never could from the ground.

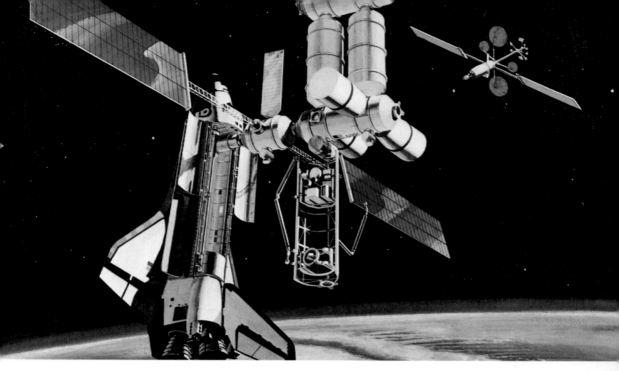

In this picture, an artist imagines a future space station with a shuttle orbiter on a resupply mission docked to it. Large, winglike solar panels stick out on both sides of several modules. The modules provide living and working quarters for six to eight people.

Scientists can experiment, too, with weightlessness. Many questions need to be answered. How does a spider spin its web when there's no gravity? How do crystals grow in space? What new materials could be made in an orbiting factory?

People living and working in space can achieve far more than simple robot satellites. They can do more difficult tasks and make better observations. People can make decisions, or fix things if they go wrong.

For space exploration, the next great step will be to build orbiting space stations. These "workshops" at the edge of space will be designed so that scientists can carry out experiments there. Already, the United States and the Soviet Union have taken steps toward this goal.

In 1973, America launched its **Skylab** space station

In the twenty-first century, space colonies such as the one shown in this artist's picture may be home for thousands of people. Some scientists have suggested that a space colony could be built in an orbit between the earth and the moon.

and sent three separate crews to live in it. These astronauts spent a total of 171 days in Skylab. Within 10 years, the United States may have a space station that's always lived in. It will be built from pieces carried into space by the shuttle.

The Soviet Union also has plans for a long-lasting space station. In 1982, **cosmonauts** Berezovoy and Lebedev broke the record for the longest stay in space when they spent 211 days aboard *Salyut 6*. In the future, the Soviet Union will launch bigger space stations with more docking ports for visiting spacecraft and supply ships.

After space stations, perhaps space colonies will be next. Even now, scientists are designing huge orbiting structures, several miles long, that may be home for thousands of people in the next century.

The inside of a large space colony might look like this artist's picture. An earthlike gravity could be produced by long, rotating cylinders such as the ones shown on the left-hand page. Inside them the space colony could be made to look like places on earth.

The great colonies in the sky would have factories able to make new metals, glasses, and other materials. They would run solar power stations that could beam down extra energy for use on earth.

Materials for building the colonies could be mined on the moon. Or, they could come from asteroids—great rocks that fly through space and sometimes pass close to the earth. All the colonies' energy would be supplied by the sun, whose power would be captured by large **solar collectors.**

It's hard to imagine living in space, hundreds of miles above the earth. But what will it be like to explore other parts of the sun's kingdom and worlds quite different from our own?

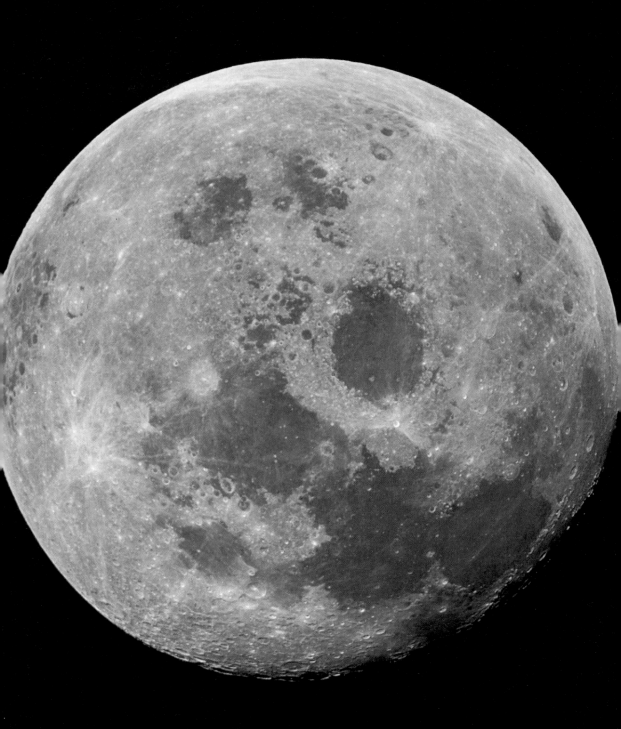

THE MOON, OUR NEAREST NEIGHBOR IN SPACE

3 Worlds Beyond Earth

We live in a fascinating part of space called the **solar system.** At its center is the sun, a yellow **star.** Around the sun are nine orbiting planets, and around the planets are dozens of orbiting moons.

The Closest World

Just 239,000 miles (384,000 kilometers) away from earth is the moon. It is our nearest neighbor in space and, for this reason, was the first to be explored by spacecraft.

In January 1959, the Soviet Union's *Luna 1* flew by the moon. It was the first spacecraft ever to escape the earth's gravity. Then came *Luna 2*, the first craft to crash into another world, and *Luna 3*, the first to photograph the moon's far side.

The moon was used as a testing ground for robot craft that might later explore more distant worlds. *Luna 9* became the first successful "soft-lander," a spaceship that uses rockets to brake its fall. *Luna 10* became the first spacecraft to orbit a world beyond earth.

On September 12, 1970, the Soviet Union launched *Luna 16*, a "sample-return" probe. Twelve days later, the little craft landed back on earth with a precious 3½-ounce cargo of moon dust! It was followed by *Luna 17* and its ro-

On July 20, 1969, astronaut Edwin Aldrin climbed down the ladder of the lunar module *Eagle.* Astronaut Neil Armstrong, already standing on the moon's surface, took this historic photograph.

bot "rover," a wheeled vehicle that rumbled 6½ miles (10½ kilometers) across the moon's dusty plains.

America, too, joined the race to the moon. With **Ranger, Surveyor,** and **Lunar Orbiter** craft, the U.S. space program prepared for a lunar landing by the astronauts of *Apollo 11.*

On July 20, 1969, Neil Armstrong and Edwin Aldrin, aboard their lunar module *Eagle,* touched down on the Sea of Tranquility. For more than two hours they walked on the moon's surface, setting up experiments and collecting rocks.

Armstrong and Aldrin were followed by astronauts on five other Apollo missions, each more daring than the one before. In all, 842 pounds (382 kilograms) of moon rocks were brought back to earth. From them scientists

This is an artist's view of a future mining town on the moon. In the foreground a small transportation spacecraft waits for lift-off.

have learned about the makeup and history of our nearest neighbor in space.

The last lunar spacecraft, *Luna 24*, blasted off from the moon on August 19, 1976. Since then no one has tried to go back. Still, the moon may play an important part in future space missions.

With its lack of atmosphere, the moon would be an ideal place from which to observe the universe. With its low gravity, it would also make a good launch site for spacecraft traveling deeper into the solar system.

We know, thanks to the Apollo missions, that people living on a moon base could get all their supplies of water and **oxygen** from the lunar soil. We know, too, that the moon is rich in metals. These could be used for building spaceships or even giant, Earth-orbiting space colonies.

But before we return there, we may choose to explore farther from home. Already, our robot craft have shown us some of the amazing worlds waiting for us in other parts of the solar system.

The Innermost Worlds

Twenty-six million miles away, at its closest approach, is Venus. Because it is nearer the sun than Earth, Venus is a much hotter planet. Its surface is always hidden beneath a thick layer of bright clouds.

Seen through telescopes on Earth, Venus is just a fuzzy, white ball. But visiting spacecraft have begun to uncover the secrets that lie hidden beneath its thick, hot layers of deadly clouds.

Several spacecraft have carried "entry probes" to

In this picture, an artist imagines how the Venus Radar Mapper probe might look as it approaches the dense, hot, thick clouds that make up Venus's atmosphere.

Venus. Some of these have parachuted onto the planet's burning hot surface. There they found a dim, rocky, steamy wilderness. Others have floated in the atmosphere, sampling the clouds of **carbon dioxide** and **sulfuric acid.** None, so far, have survived for more than an hour. But in the future, tougher probes will be sent that can withstand the terrible atmosphere and boiling temperatures for much longer periods.

Still other spacecraft, such as the **Pioneer** Venus orbiter, have stayed above the cloud-tops and used **radar** to look at Venus's surface. In 1988, a special Venus Radar Mapper probe may be launched to study the planet's hidden surface in more detail.

One of the Venus probes, *Mariner 10,* also went on to explore **Mercury,** the closest planet to the sun. Nothing

29

Mariner 10 took this photo of the heavily cratered, sunbaked surface of Mercury.

until then was known about Mercury's surface. But *Mariner 10*'s cameras showed it in fantastic detail. Tiny, sun-baked Mercury is a world that's cratered and wrinkled. Its sizzling hot days and freezing cold nights, and its lack of air or water, make it a place almost as unfriendly as Venus.

Mission to Mars

Beyond the moon, the first planet that people may visit is Mars. Fourth in distance from the sun, it's a much smaller world than our own. Mars is much colder and has only a very thin atmosphere of carbon dioxide. Yet, of all the planets in the solar system, it's the one most like Earth.

Our best views of the "red planet" have come from

This photograph, taken by a Viking lander, shows the brightly-colored surface of the "red planet."

Mariner 9, in 1971, and the two **Viking** spacecraft, in 1976. *Mariner 9,* from its orbit above Mars, surprised everyone by discovering dried-up river beds.

The twin Viking orbiters sent back even better pictures. These added to our knowledge of the old river channels, giant volcanoes, immense canyons, wispy atmosphere, and icy poles of Mars. They showed us, too, the tiny, potato-shaped Martian moons, *Phobos* and *Deimos.* Both moons are probably captured asteroids.

The Viking landers, meanwhile, dropped gently to the Martian surface. Using parachutes as wide as a football field, they fell slowly through the thin atmosphere. Again, they measured the makeup of the atmosphere. Once they were safely on the ground, they searched for signs of life, but found none. From the surface, they sent back beautiful pictures of red-stained, rocky deserts and a pink, dusty Martian sky.

In the future, people will land on Mars. In time, humans may build a space colony there. We may also send other robot probes to bring back a sample of Mars's soil or to roam across its surface.

Moons, Rings, and Icy Giants

Farther from the sun than Mars lie the strange, lonely worlds of the outer solar system. First comes a rocky ring of "mini-planets"—the **asteroid belt.** Then the four icy giants—Jupiter, Saturn, Uranus, and Neptune—loom large and bright, faraway from the sun's life-giving heat and light. Most distant of all, 3½ billion miles out, is tiny **Pluto.**

Jupiter's whirling orange, yellow, and brown clouds stand out in this *Viking 2* photograph of the solar system's largest planet.

Spacecraft have only just begun to explore these more distant worlds. Our first probe to cross the asteroid belt, *Pioneer 10*, was launched in March 1972, and reached Jupiter in December 1973. It was followed a year later by *Pioneer 11*, which also went on to fly by Saturn.

Then came the much larger spacecraft, *Voyager 1* and *Voyager 2*, launched in 1977. Both skimmed by Jupiter and were hurled on by its gravity towards Saturn. The pictures sent back by the two Voyagers are among the most amazing space photographs ever seen.

They show Jupiter's whirling orange, yellow, and brown clouds in fine detail. On the night side of the planet, they show huge electrical storms.

Jupiter isn't a place that people will ever try to land on. Its great, 88,000-mile-wide globe has a thick atmo-

Voyager 1 took this close-up picture of Jupiter's moon, Io. An erupting volcano stands out against the blackness of space along the curving edge of this active moon.

sphere of **hydrogen, helium, methane,** and **ammonia.** Below these thick clouds is a vast sea of liquid hydrogen. Only deep inside, where the pressure is unbearable, is there a hard, rocky core.

Perhaps one of Jupiter's many moons would be a better place to explore. For the first time, thanks to the Voyager missions, we have seen what the surfaces of some of these moons are like.

Our next chance to study Jupiter close up will be the **Galileo** probe. Due for launch in 1985, it will have two parts. The first is an orbiter. The second is an entry probe, which will send back information as it drops into the giant planet's thick, swirling clouds.

After flying by Jupiter, the two Voyagers went on to explore Saturn. This planet has the largest and most

This is an artist's view of a future scientific outpost on Ganymede, Jupiter's largest moon. Such an outpost could be used as a base to study and explore the outer worlds in the solar system.

beautiful set of rings in the sun's kingdom. The space-craft showed that Saturn's rings are not as smooth as most scientists had expected. Instead, they are more like the grooves of a record, with thousands of ringlets separated by narrow gaps.

The twin Voyagers also took a close look at many of Saturn's twenty or so known moons. *Voyager 1* passed within just 4,033 miles (6,490 kilometers) of the largest, **Titan.** It found that this orange-haze-covered moon has a thick atmosphere which, like Earth's, is made mainly of **nitrogen.** Scientists would now like to send a special probe to Titan to study it more closely.

Three of the spacecraft that have flown by Jupiter and Saturn are on their way out of the solar system. The fourth, *Voyager 2*, is also due to leave the sun's kingdom.

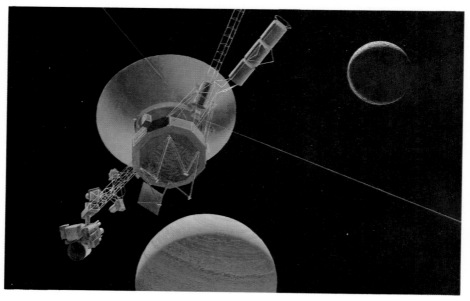

In this picture an artist shows *Voyager 2* looking back toward Neptune after flying by the planet in August 1989.

First, though, it will fly near Uranus in 1986, and then Neptune in 1989.

By the end of the 1980s, we will have seen every planet in the solar system close up, except one. Only Pluto, and its strange moon, **Charon,** will remain unexplored.

We have plans, too, to visit a smaller member of the sun's kingdom. In 1986, **Halley's comet** will pass by us on its 76-year journey around the sun. Five spacecraft—two from Japan, two from the Soviet Union, and one from a group of European nations—will be sent out to meet it. The European probe, **Giotto,** is especially exciting. Scientists hope that it will get to within about 300 miles (500 kilometers) of the comet. From there its instruments may be able to glimpse the tiny frozen "nucleus" buried deep inside.

An artist's view of a spacecraft passing close by Halley's comet. Five spacecraft will be sent on missions to study the comet when it speeds around the sun in 1986.

It will take many years to explore all the strange places in the solar system. But even then, our great adventure will have barely begun.

AN ARTIST'S VIEW OF AN INTERSTELLAR SPACECRAFT

4 Towards the Stars

Light, traveling at 186,000 miles per second (300,000 kilometers per second), takes about five hours to cross the vast distance between Pluto and Earth. In other words, Pluto is roughly five **light-hours** away.

The nearest star beyond the sun, Proxima Centauri, is 4¼ **light-years** away, a distance of 25 **trillion** miles (40 trillion kilometers). If the whole solar system were the size of a 25-cent coin, the nearest star would still be the length of a football field away!

The stars make even the great distances to the outer planets seem small. Will we ever, then, be able to reach them by spacecraft?

The answer is yes, but not in our lifetimes. In fact, *Pioneer 10* and *11*, along with *Voyager 1* and *2*, are already heading out of the solar system and into interstellar space. They will take a very long time to reach the nearest stars, though. *Pioneer 10*, for instance, will fly by the faint red star Ross 248, 10 1/3 light-years from home, in about the year A.D. 270,000! Even then, the craft will not be near enough to the star to explore any new planets around it.

True interstellar spacecraft must be able to reach the nearest stars in far less time than *Pioneer 10*. To do this, they will require new kinds of rocket engines that can boost them to speeds far greater than those of present-day probes. Once they arrive in a new star system, they will have to explore without any help from earth. Even radio signals, traveling at the speed of light, take years to cross the great distances between stars.

Many ideas have been suggested for interstellar spacecraft. One of the best came from a team of scientists and engineers of the British Interplanetary Society. Called Project Daedalus, it's a design for a robot craft that would travel to Barnard's Star, about six light-years away.

The starship's journey, at a top speed of 22,000 miles per second (36,000 kilometers per second), would take 50 years. It would be powered by **fusion,** the same process that makes the sun shine and give off heat.

The launch of the space shuttle. To explore the worlds that lie beyond our solar system, we will need to create interstellar spacecraft that travel at the speed of light or even faster.

Daedalus would carry telescopes, cameras, and other instruments for making measurements on its long voyage. It would also carry a number of smaller probes for exploring any planets that it might find around Barnard's Star. All of the decisions required during the mission would be made by on-board computers.

Following such a mission, we may wish to visit the stars ourselves. Like the starship *Enterprise* of *Star Trek*, travelers from earth may one day cross interstellar space at speeds we can only imagine today.

Oddly enough, time changes on a spacecraft traveling close to the speed of light. In fact, scientists believe that a person on such a mission would age much more slowly than people on earth. For this reason, in the future it may be possible to cross the entire **galaxy**—a distance of 100,000 light-years—within a single lifetime.

In centuries to come, we may find ways to go even faster than light. Then we could hop from star to star as easily as we fly between cities on earth today.

No one really knows where we are going in space. But one thing seems clear. For us and for future generations, a great adventure and amazing sights lie waiting as we begin to explore the strange worlds around us.

Appendix A:
Discover For Yourself

1. *Orbit Your Own Satellite*

The speed at which satellites must go around the earth depends on the height of their orbits. A satellite 300 miles (500 kilometers) above our planet must travel at about 17,000 miles per hour to stay in orbit. A satellite 1,000 miles (1,670 kilometers) above the earth must travel at about 16,000 miles per hour. The lower the orbit, the faster a satellite must go.

What would happen if we suddenly slowed down a satellite in its path around the earth? What would happen if we suddenly speeded it up? To find the answers, all you need is a plastic bowl and a marble. The bottom of the bowl represents the earth, the sides of the bowl represent the space around the earth, and the marble represents a satellite.

Start by moving the bowl so that the marble "orbits" around the inside wall of the bowl. Getting this to work will take practice. For just like a real satellite, the marble has to go at exactly the right speed to stay in its orbit.

Now, move the bowl more slowly. Stop the bowl completely. What happens? Real satellites fall back to earth, too, if their speed becomes too low.

Next, move the bowl faster, and faster. What happens? A satellite that goes too fast spirals outwards, and may even escape earth's gravity altogether.

2. *Plan a Trip to Another World*

Choose a planet, moon, or other world in the solar system that you'd like to explore. Then, find out as much as you can about it. Make a scrapbook of your chosen world and fill it with facts, figures, drawings, paintings, and newspaper or magazine clippings. What would it be like to stand on the surface of your world? Can you imagine finding any forms of life there? Use this and other books on space to help you find the answers.

How long will it take you to reach your world? Appendix C gives travel times to the planets, and some other space objects, for a rocket going by the shortest possible route at a steady 25,000 miles per hour.

How much will you weigh when you arrive? The answer depends on the size and mass of your world. Look at the astronaut weight chart in Appendix B. Find your "Earth-weight" in the shaded column, and then read off the row of numbers to the right to discover your weight on some other worlds. How heavy would you be on Jupiter? How heavy on Pluto?

Your rocket must be powerful enough to blast off from your world when you are ready to leave. It must be able to go fast enough to escape the gravity of the world so that it can return to Earth. Some planets, such as Jupiter and Saturn, have strong pulls of gravity. A spacecraft would need to go very fast indeed to escape from their surfaces. Other, smaller worlds, such as the moon or Pluto, have weaker pulls of gravity. Check Appendix D to find out the speed you would need to go in order to escape from the main worlds of the solar system.

Appendix B:
Astronaut Weight Chart
(All Weights Given to the Nearest Pound)

EARTH	MOON	MERCURY	VENUS	MARS	JUPITER
50	8	19	45	19	132
55	9	21	50	21	145
60	10	23	54	23	158
65	11	25	59	25	172
70	12	27	63	27	185
75	12	28	68	28	198
80	13	30	72	30	211
85	14	32	77	32	224
90	15	34	81	34	238
95	16	36	86	36	251
100	17	38	90	38	264
105	17	40	95	40	277
110	18	42	99	42	290
115	19	44	104	44	304
120	20	46	108	46	317
125	21	47	113	47	330
130	21	49	117	49	343
135	22	51	122	51	356
140	23	53	126	53	370
145	24	55	131	55	383
150	25	57	135	57	396

SATURN	URANUS	NEPTUNE	PLUTO	SUN	GANYMEDE	CERES
58	58	60	2	1395	7	2
64	64	66	3	1534	8	2
70	70	72	3	1674	9	2
75	76	78	3	1813	10	3
81	82	84	3	1953	10	3
87	88	90	4	2092	11	3
93	94	96	4	2232	12	3
99	99	102	4	2371	13	3
104	105	108	4	2511	13	4
110	111	114	5	2650	14	4
116	117	120	5	2790	15	4
122	123	126	5	2929	16	4
127	129	132	5	3069	16	4
133	135	138	6	3208	17	5
139	140	144	6	3348	18	5
145	146	150	6	3487	19	5
151	152	156	6	3627	19	5
157	158	162	7	3766	20	5
162	164	168	7	3906	21	6
168	170	174	7	4045	22	6
174	175	180	7	4185	22	6

Appendix C: Travel Times
from Earth to Various Worlds
(at a Steady 25,000 Miles Per Hour)

Place	Travel Time
moon	9½ hours
Venus	39 days
Mars	62 days
Mercury	81 days
sun	5 months
Ceres, the largest asteroid	7½ months
Jupiter	20 months
Ganymede, the largest moon	20 months
Saturn	3½ years
Uranus	8 years
Neptune	12 years
Pluto	16 years
Nearest star, after the sun	117,000 years

Appendix D: Rocket Speeds
Speeds At Which A Rocket Must Go to Escape From Various Worlds

Place	Escape Speed (Miles Per Hour)
moon	5,328
Mercury	9,612
Venus	23,184
Earth	25,020
Mars	11,268
Jupiter	134,748
Saturn	72,180
Uranus	50,328
Neptune	53,460
Pluto	2,707
sun	1,381,608
Ganymede	6,228
Ceres	1,410

Appendix E: Space Exploration—
A Possible Time-Table for the Future

Date	Event (Events in shaded area are scheduled; the others are not)
1985	Launch of Galileo orbiter and entry probe to Jupiter (USA)
1986	Five probes fly by Halley's comet (Europe, USSR, Japan) *Voyager 2* reaches Uranus
1987	Space Telescope in orbit
1988	Venus Radar Mapper goes into orbit around Venus Galileo probe arrives at Jupiter
1989	*Voyager 2* arrives at Neptune
1990	Mars orbiter
1991	Titan orbiter/entry probe Saturn orbiter
1992	Asteroid fly-by probe
1993	Kepler orbiter to Mars (Europe)
1994	Permanent space stations in earth orbit (USA and USSR) Comet sample-return probe
1995	Mars sample-return probe/rover Venus soft-lander probe/rover

Date	Event
2000	Ganymede orbiter/soft-lander Pluto and Charon fly-by probe
2010	First human mission to Mars Asteroid soft-lander/sample-return probe
2020	Permanent base on the moon
2030	Launch of first interstellar probe
2040	First passenger trips to the moon
2050	First space colony
2100	Permanent base in the outer Solar System (perhaps on Ganymede)
2150	First human mission to a nearby star (Alpha Centauri, Barnard's Star)
2250	First base around another star
2500	Exploration of many nearby stars
3000	Colonies around many nearby stars

Appendix F:
Amateur Astronomy Groups
in the United States,
Canada, and Great Britain

For information or resource materials about the subjects covered in this book, contact your local astronomy group, science museum, or planetarium. You may also write to one of the national amateur astronomy groups listed below.

United States

The Astronomical League
Donald Archer,
  Executive Secretary
P.O. Box 12821
Tucson, Arizona 85732

American Association of
  Variable Star Astronomers
187 Concord Avenue
Cambridge, Massachusetts 02138

Great Britain

Junior Astronomical Society
58 Vaughan Gardens
Ilford
Essex IG1 3PD England

British Astronomical Assoc.
Burlington House
Piccadilly
London W1V 0NL England

Canada

The Royal Astronomical Society of Canada
La Société Royale d'Astronomie du Canada
Rosemary Freeman, Executive Secretary
136 Dupont Street
Toronto, Ontario M5R 1V2 Canada

Glossary

ammonia—a poisonous gas found in the atmospheres of the outer planets: Jupiter, Saturn, Uranus, and Neptune

Apollo—America's project to land astronauts on the moon. Altogether, six Apollos reached the moon, beginning with *Apollo 11* in July 1969, and ending with *Apollo 17* in December 1972

asteroids—large rocks, from less than a mile across to several hundred miles across, that go around the sun. See *asteroid belt*

asteroid belt—the region, between the orbits of Mars and Jupiter, in which most of the asteroids are found

astronomy satellite—a human-made satellite that carries instruments into space to study distant parts of the universe

atmosphere—the layer of gases above the surface of a world

billion—a thousand million. Written as 1,000,000,000

black hole—a star, or other object, that has fallen in on itself so that not even light can escape from the space around it

carbon dioxide—a gas found in the atmospheres of Venus and Mars, and to a lesser extent, that of Earth. It is the gas that plants breathe

Charon—Pluto's only known moon. At 800 miles in diameter, it's almost half as big as Pluto itself

comets—small chunks of rock and ice that go around the sun. As they approach the sun, they may grow tails that stretch out behind

them for millions of miles

communications satellite—a human-made satellite that beams messages such as telephone and television signals from one place on earth to another

core—the small, heavy, central part of a planet or moon

cosmonaut—a Russian astronaut

Daedalus—the name of a starship designed by British scientists in the 1970s. Daedalus could be built in the middle of the next century and launched on a 50-year voyage to nearby Barnard's Star

Deimos—the smaller of Mars's two moons. It is only a few miles across and is probably a captured asteroid

earth surveillance satellite—a human-made satellite that studies either the earth's surface or its atmosphere. See *resource satellite* and *weather satellite*

Explorer—an American series of space probes designed to do various science experiments in earth orbit

fusion—a way of making large amounts of energy by turning simple, light substances such as hydrogen into more complicated, heavier substances at very high temperatures

Galaxy—the great "Island Universe"—a collection of more than 100 billion stars—in which we live

Galileo—an American spacecraft due to be

launched towards Jupiter in 1985. It is made up of an orbiter and an entry probe for studying Jupiter at close range

gamma rays—the most powerful waves of energy known. They are much like ordinary light, but are made only in regions of space where a lot of energy is concentrated

geostationary orbit—a special orbit, about 22,200 miles (35,700 kilometers) above the earth's equator, used by communications satellites to stay above the same point on earth

Giotto—a spacecraft, built by several European countries, that will journey to within a few hundred miles of Halley's comet in 1986

Halley's comet—the brightest comet that can be seen regularly from earth. It passes close to the sun once every 76 years and will be seen again in 1986

helium—a light gas found in the atmospheres of the giant outer planets

hydrogen—the most common substance making up the outer planets: Jupiter, Saturn, Uranus, and Neptune

infrared—the kind of waves that carry heat. They are given off by all warm objects on earth and in space

interstellar—a word meaning "between the stars"

Jupiter—the largest planet in the solar system. It is 89,000 miles in diameter and made mostly of hydrogen, helium, methane, and ammonia

light-hour—the distance light travels in an hour. See *light-year*

light-year—the distance light travels in a year—roughly 6 trillion miles (9½ trillion kilometers)

Luna—the Soviet series of spacecraft that explored the moon between 1959 and 1976

Lunar Orbiter—a series of American spacecraft that mapped every part of the moon from orbit and prepared the way for the Apollo landings

Mariner—a series of American spacecraft designed for exploration of the planets. Various Mariner probes have studied Mercury, Venus, and Mars from close up in space

Mars—The fourth planet from the sun and the one most like Earth. Mars used to have rivers, but much of its water today is frozen into its polar ice caps

Mercury—the closest planet to the sun and one of the smallest and hottest. It has no atmosphere, no water, very hot days and very cold nights

methane—a poisonous gas found in the atmospheres of the outer planets

million—a thousand thousand. Written as 1,000,000

moon—earth's only natural satellite. It is 2,160 miles (3,475 kilometers) in diameter and orbits at a distance of 239,000 miles (384,000 kilometers)

Neptune—the eighth planet from the sun at a distance of 2.795 billion miles. *Voyager 2* is due to

pass close by it in 1989
nitrogen—the most
common gas in Earth's
atmosphere. It is found in
large amounts on only one
other world, Saturn's giant
moon, Titan

orbit—the path that an
object follows as it moves
around another object.
Planets, for example, follow
orbits around the sun;
moons and artificial
satellites follow orbits
around planets
oxygen—the gas in earth's
atmosphere that humans
need to breathe

Phobos—the larger of
Mars's two moons. Like
Deimos, it is probably a
captured asteroid
Pioneer—a series of
American planetary
spacecraft. Pioneers have

been used to explore Venus
as well as the more distant
worlds, Jupiter and Saturn.
Pioneer 10 became the first
probe ever to leave the solar
system
planet—a world, usually
several thousand miles or
more in diameter, that goes
around a star. The sun has
nine planets. Other stars
almost certainly have
orbiting planets, too
Pluto—the smallest and
most distant planet. It will
be many years before a
spacecraft explores Pluto or
its strange moon, Charon
probe—a spacecraft
designed to follow a certain
path, gather information,
and send it back to
scientists on earth

radar—a method for
finding objects, and their
distances, by bouncing

radio signals off them

Ranger—the first series of American probes to explore the moon. Only three Rangers were successful, but these sent back thousands of photographs before crashing into the moon's surface

resource satellite—an earth surveillance satellite that studies crops, forests, supplies of important fuels, minerals, and metals, and other things on the earth's surface

Salyut—a series of Soviet space stations that may be visited by crews of cosmonauts for periods of several weeks or months. They will eventually lead to larger space stations that are lived in all the time

satellite—the name given to any object that circles around and is captured by the gravity of a larger object. Satellites may be either artificial (human-made) or natural. The earth's only natural satellite is the moon

Saturn—the second largest planet and the one with the most beautiful set of rings in the solar system

Skylab—the first American space station. Launched in 1973, it was made from a converted Saturn 5 rocket fuel tank, 10 stores high

solar collector—a device for trapping heat from the sun and using it to supply energy

solar system—the sun, plus all of the objects that go around it, including planets, moons, asteroids, and comets

space colony—a "city in space." In the future, space colonies may be built in earth orbit that have their own factories, power stations, and living spaces for thousands of people

Spacelab—a European space laboratory that can be carried and put into orbit by the space shuttle. Its missions include studying the earth, the sun, and more distant regions of space

space shuttle—America's latest, reusable spacecraft. With the help of attached rockets, it blasts into earth orbit. Then, having launched or repaired satellites, it returns to earth like an airplane

space station—an orbiting satellite where scientist-astronauts live and study. See *Skylab, Salyut,* and *Spacelab*

Space Telescope—a large telescope that will be put into earth orbit by the shuttle in 1986

Sputnik—an early Soviet series of earth satellites. *Sputnik 1*—the first spacecraft of all—was put into orbit in October 1957

star—a large ball of gases that shines by its own light and heat

sulfuric acid—a dangerous substance found in the cloud-tops of Venus

Surveyor—a series of American spacecraft that soft-landed on the moon in the late 1960s

Titan—Saturn's largest moon and the only world in the solar system, apart from Earth, having an atmosphere mainly of nitrogen

trillion—a thousand billion. Written as 1,000,000,000,000

ultraviolet—the type of

rays that cause sunburn. They are given off in especially large amounts by very hot stars

Uranus—the seventh planet from the sun at a distance of 1.783 billion miles (2.870 billion kilometers). *Voyager 2* will pass close by it in January 1986

Venus—the planet that comes closest to earth. It is covered by a thick atmosphere of carbon dioxide and is the hottest of all the worlds in the solar system

Viking—the name of the two American spacecraft that explored Mars in 1977. Both Vikings were made up of an orbiter and a lander

Voyager—the name of the two large spacecraft that flew by Jupiter and Saturn between 1979 and 1981

weather satellite—an earth surveillance satellite that studies storms and other weather patterns in the earth's atmosphere

weightlessness—the effect of feeling no weight when in orbit, or when moving at a steady speed through space. It is also called "zero gravity"

X rays—powerful waves of energy. Although similar to light, they are made only in parts of space where there's a lot of energy or a very high temperature

Suggested Reading

Joels, Kerry Mark, and Kennedy, Gregory P. *The Space Shuttle Operator's Manual.* New York: Ballantine, 1982.
Takes you on board the shuttle and makes you the astronaut. This book includes mission checklists and flight plans, as well as a complete description of the shuttle itself. (Intermediate to Advanced)

Poynter, Margaret, and Lane, Arthur L. *Voyager: the Story of a Space Mission.* New York: Atheneum, 1981.
A behind-the-scenes look at one of the most successful space exploration projects to date—the Voyager missions to the outer planets. Learn about what goes into such a project, about the achievements made possible by a group of men and women scientists, and about the Voyager spacecraft themselves.

Sharpe, Mitchell R. *"It is I, Sea Gull."* New York: Thomas Y. Crowell, 1975.
Tells the story of Valentina Tereshkova, Russian cosmonaut, and the first woman in space. (Intermediate)

Trefil, James S. *Living in Space.* New York: Charles Scribner's Sons, 1981.
Why should we build space colonies? What would it be like to live in one? Discover the answers in this book, and learn more about the fascinating possibilities for your future in space.

✳ **Index**